My Life In Words

Roberta Brown

My Life In Words © 2022 Roberta Brown

All rights reserved.

No part of this publication may be reproduced, stored in a retrieval system, or transmitted, in any form or by any means, electronic, mechanical, photocopying, recording or otherwise, without the prior written permission of the presenters.

Roberta Brown asserts the moral right to be identified as author of this work.

Presentation by *BookLeaf Publishing*

Web: www.bookleafpub.com

E-mail: info@bookleafpub.com

ISBN: 978-93-95088-22-0

First edition 2022

DEDICATION

I dedicate this book to whoever needs to be seen, heard, loved and respected.

I hope others will learn from my past difficulties and know that it is only when you learn to value your own life that you can spend time with those who are in alignment with your core beliefs.

You are never alone and you are always good enough, no matter what. Turning wounds into wisdom and tragedies into triumphs has been my philosophy in moving forward.

We all deserve to live a peaceful life and so I dedicate this book to all the women who held and continue to hold space for me. If you remember one thing, let it be this. 'The opposite of belonging is fitting in'

Never lose yourself trying to fit in, no matter how hard this is.

Much love

Roberta

ACKNOWLEDGEMENT

I have to thank Lorna Humphreys, my amazing illustrator for my book Tallulah who nominated me for this challenge. I dedicate this book to my sons, Sol, Sam and Ben, you have all taught me a great deal in very different ways. My Furry children, Dolly, Betty, Mabel and Barney, my Golden Doodles who have given me a reason to wake up each day. However, the one person I owe my life to is me. I have overcome obstacles that even astound me. So, this is a thank you to me, I have finally seen I am worthy of love and I am proud of my life and all that I am. To my small circle of women friends, you know who you are. Finally to my mother, the woman who gave me life, even through the thick and thin you are my lovely mum, my best friend and my everything and I thank you for everything you have tried to teach me .

PREFACE

Here I am at 53, finally these are some of my life events using my own words. Words can empower or destroy and I am going to take you into a glimpse of my world with the gift of my writing.
You will read my feelings and the words may or may not resonate with you in some or all of the poems. I have lived a life so far, of great love, loss, abuse, pain, joy, heartbreak and freedom, like many of us.

I will use the wisdom I have gained to hopefully inspire you to live a wholehearted life. Each poem is based on true life events and have been and still are lived experiences as I travel on this wiggly path called life. My purpose in this world is to help connect people to themselves. I realize I have lived more years than I have left to live so I intend to make the most of each moment by aligning my personality with my purpose.

Painful Heart

Anxiety and Me

The silence was lonely
My aching heart cried
And wherever I went
There was nowhere to hide

Wherever I am you just won't leave
Anxiety, fear, there is no reprieve
When fear pays a visit I can't see the door

You're blocking my exit
My pain feels raw

For 53 years you have haunted my mind
Sometimes when I wake, I really do dread
The days when you manage to enter my head

Like a parasite,you stay too long
I didn't invite you -
You don't belong
Now go, just leave me alone
I don't need you, I'm fine on my own

Anxiety, you are stealing my days

Fuck you, with your evil ways

I'm sick of you I really am
You cause me so much pain
I try so hard but yet right now,
I feel it's all in vain
As I hide in my home and have nothing to say
To people who call and text me each day

I'm scared, so scared
Like a child I once knew
I thought I had finally learnt what to do

And I have, so leave
I am stronger than this
53 years - now you're taking the piss

Yes I feel low and long to be strong
But to think this is it
Now that would be be wrong

For I am strong with inner light
The pain feels dark just like the night

I know I will rise when my heart starts to heal
And yes I'm still me
That, you can't steal

Shorter Days

As the nights draw in and the sun leaves at four
I have longed for short days like never before

The moon lights the sky with a bright misty ray
And I feel better with a shorter day
I know that the hours are the same for everyone
But winter days allow me to rest in the sun

Even in the winter, when the days feel cold and
short
I'm more awake and happier inside my cosy fort

I've been thinking often why I like a shorter day
And finally I know - and this is what I say

When you've had trauma and the day doesn't
end
You crave for nighttime, for sleep is your friend
 I have yearned to sleep my mind away
Where I dream of my Dad and how we did play

Summertime filled with sunny spells and
carefree days
People laughing endlessly - children splashing in
the waves

All I can think of is not long now
Winter is coming and I whisper WOW
The leaves start dancing and fall with grace

I hear their crunch and smile at the clues
The orange and red of the autumn hues
How I breathe a sigh of relief
When days are shorter so is your grief

For nobody sees the ache in my chest or the pain
that I hold
This is the reason I love to feel cold
The winter allows my pain to go numb
As I question my life and what will become

 I hide behind my jokes and my raucous laugh
Where no one can see my half broken heart
The winter will come and if I'm lucky the rain
And I will sit patiently just me and my pain

The Congo

How can children starve to death
In this world where we reside?
The Congo calls out loud to us
But the west just seems to hide

I watched the news and saw their fate
Their faces void of love
Where is god in all of this
That being up above

Babies strapped to mothers backs
No milk for them to grow

But surely in this world we live
They'll have somewhere to go

But where, how, when and why?
I ask as if I'm there
I'm only ten but my eyes tell
My heart inside to care

Tragedy is all I sense
I'm like a prisoner just set free
I'm not hungry, I'm not scared
Why them, not me?

Wicked wasteful war I say
To men in suits who lead our land
Can't you hear the Congo pray
Stand up, hold out your hand

Feed the children, mums and dads
Give them back their rights
Imagine they were your blood
You soon would start to fight

Monoculture

Why act like sheep and follow the crowd
Do we think our beliefs are not allowed
Why do we live our life in one way
The way we were taught day after day

Surely we're free unique and can share
The qualities of our DNA flair
Born to a mother and raised in a place
Knowing only this life and watching this race
To the people I ask you where do you go

We are all on our way to our graves don't you
know

So, break free from the mould and design your
own life
You don't have to be someone's husband or wife
To fit in with society do it your way
You came into this world to learn through play

Our visit on earth is so very short
Choose what you want and how to be taught
Don't live like a sheep and follow the crowd
Use your mind - be quiet, be loud
For this is your moment - your time here on
earth
Celebrate You who arrived here at birth

Look in the mirror and and know you can trust
Yourself. Yes gosh, now that is a must

Because this really is your life - your gift
It won't be linear it will be messy and shift

From the falls we take and lessons we learn
Let your thirst for knowledge be something you
yearn
Say 'This is my life
This is my day
I'll make my rules and I'll do as I say'

Not as society says I should be
For what do they know about this person called
ME
For I am me who stands tall and strong
With focus and logic to me I belong

Monoculture that's not for me
I look at the others - the sheep and I see
A population of people who follow the crowd
I am different and for that I am proud

New York

We wake up each morning
And go about our day

Not really knowing what fate comes our way
Most of us live life as if there'll never be an end

The never ending busyness
Appears to be the trend

September 11 we all know that date
The victims that day knew not of their fate

I was at home with my sons when I saw
A terrible horror like never before

It couldn't be real - this just couldn't be
My eyes were fixated on what I could see

There are some things in life that one can't
explain
No words will ever describe the pain

The victims - their fear - they knew they would
die
Helpless, terrified, up in the sky

How now can the world still turn
What is the point - what's there to learn

20 years on, their grief is deep
Crushed hearts still crushing
So many just weep

To the victims who died on that awful day
To their family and friends whose lives are just
grey

How do you cope through the days, months and
years

I would just drown in my own salty tears
I am a mum, daughter and friend,
I treasure my life, because I know it can end

When my children pop out whether day or night
We say cheerio and always hug tight

Tomorrow's not promised our lives can just go
Tell the people you love them
Make sure they know

In Memory of 2996 beating hearts ♥
There are no words to describe what happened
to you or the families left behind

The Vessel

You were the vessel
Who gave me life

I am sorry for your sadness
For the bumpy road you ride

You made me and maybe that's the reason
I have to keep my sadness safe

You made me strong with lies
You made me turn my tragedy
Into huge triumphs

I am alive
And while I live
I will do all I can to make sure
Nobody ever feels like I once did
The introduction to love should have been you

I am beginning again on my own
A REBIRTH

My First Love

Some poems were not meant to rhyme
Instead like life, it just happens
Never in my wildest dreams
Did I ever imagine this would be life

Why I ask so many times but
You cannot hear me
So many times I begged for the scraps
You offered me

I did the best and shared the space of my body with
you
This was your home

Every heartbeat kept you alive
To grow, thrive and become unique
I don't know how my life broke
Life is guaranteed to make us fall

I have fallen for you time after time
Like a phoenix I have soared the skies
Sold my soul in the hope
You would see
Your mother, the woman who loves you
More than you'll know

One day maybe you will know
How my love became dark and my fear of death
Was no longer so terrifying
A life without you
Is no life

I breathe, walk and imagine
That the future will be different
One where my smile never ends
One where you see into my heart

For I will wait for a miracle
The first time was when you inhaled your first breath
Because of me and now, my life is blurred

I am me, who are you
Meet me one day, here on earth
Or the next life wherever that is

I choke with pain
I wait with no air
And pray that you will find me
Before it's too late
Til then
Your eyes, your small hand,
I cherished it all

You are my first love
Until the next life

I will see you there

Ukraine

Another war - unjustified - so hard to believe

That in twenty twenty two
People just sit and stare
It's not enough to listen
Action equals care
I traveled to Kharkov in two thousand and ten
Visited an orphanage, care homes and then

I arrived back in London and didn't forget
Those strangers that me and my son had met.

Their lives so different to what we knew
My son and I said what can we do

So we hired a hall and made an event
Raised lots of money
And made sure it was sent

To the families we'd met and the children in care

My heart felt heavy so it didn't stop there

I cannot believe there is still such hate
In this world we reside - what is our fate

When you turn on the news - imagine it's YOU

Then think hard as to what you can do
Because…
This really could be us one day
And then you'll hope, maybe you'll pray

All I know is I'm just me
Nobody special - but there's no I in we

I hope these words will open your eyes
We're lucky we don't have to hear the cries

Of babies, adults girls and boys
Imagine the fear at the bombs they hear

We can't imagine
And to them it's surreal
So let's try to be WE and together let's feel

Feel not ignore nor turn away
Don't switch off tvs and get on with your day
If this was your fate what would you hope

Whatever it takes in order to cope
So join me - in a mission of WE
Take out the I and less of the me

I have no answers which is why I write
To ask you to help me
Surely it's right

Morals - that is the goal
Dig deep in your mind and look in your soul.

Send some ideas and ways we can do
Less about me and less about you

Ukrainian people do not despair
 Be patient and know there are people that care.
Until then hold your loved ones near

No one deserves to live in fear.

War

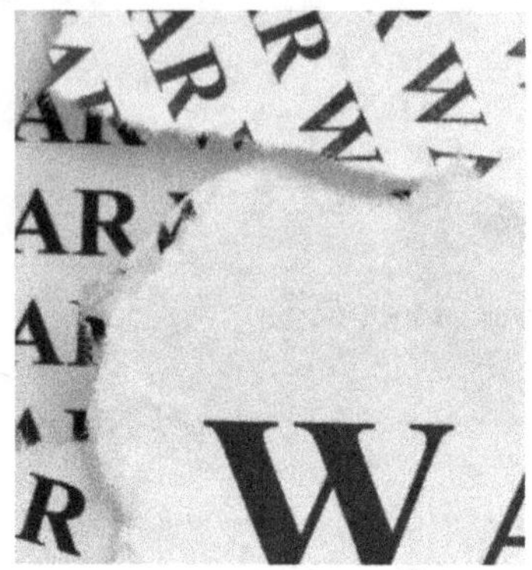

Watching, reading writing as young boys risk
their lives

Parents losing sons and husbands leaving wives

Again the hatred shocks me as lives are being
lost
Evil leaders never stop no matter what the cost

Teaching soldiers how to kill knowing they
destroy
Innocent people only wanting to have joy

Don't be silent, be brave and use your voice
The time is NOW - yes NOW, there is no other
choice

I cannot watch children die, see mothers losing
sons
This is terror at its worst, much worse than all
the guns

I'm a mum with 3 young boys and know I must
speak out
All round the world people live in fear- So this is
why I shout it out
If I'm to die for my beliefs then so it's meant to
be
But I won't sit here anymore and just be scared
old me

This is not a world I like, let's make this very
clear
Civilians even soldiers are filled with ghastly
fear
Crazy fundamentalists, is this your gods plan

The universe is good.. we must do what we can

Earth is our land and it shall remain
Teach the young kindness, war only brings pain
I sit awake and want to go and help all those that
grieve
Hold their hands and be there and help them to
believe

That maybe somehow, somewhere, something
good will come
But for sure it never will if the world will just be
dumb

Sitting back in silence that's what most of us do
There are very frightened people - imagine it
was YOU

Believe

Try to imagine life before birth
There's so much more
Than life on earth

Imagine when we leave this place
Life goes on somewhere in space

When people die, they start anew
Believe in this to help you through
Shed your tears to help you grieve
And try so hard to believe

We are given good deeds to fulfill from birth
They have to be done here on earth

As soon as we're finished, God moves us on
The people behind think we have gone

The good who pass, their deeds were done
A new life for them has already begun
The young whose soul is unique and kind
Are taken fast, leaving us behind

Words are cheap at a time like this
Hurt can have no end
Believe if you can and given time
Your heart will start to mend

School Memories 2004
Written For Sol

When I was two, I came to this school
The teachers were friendly, the place was cool
Off I went into class two playing with paints and
sticking with glue

I started staying til the afternoon
I learnt about the man in the moon
The children were noisy, but I didn't mind
The teachers gave cuddles, they were really kind

Soon I went into class three
I had perfected my pooh and my wee
I grew much bigger every day
laughing and learning with time to play

Uniform time when I turned four
And now I learnt a whole lot more
I was happy, it was easy to see
I could more than counting to three

My mum got into trouble, she forgot to bring my
hat
The lady at the front said' we cant be having that
School life was fun, even though there were
rules

But that's how it is with all other schools
Six blue and am learning new things every day
My teachers are great but mum looks at me in
her special way
She says I have to leave soon and tells me she'll
cry
I put my arm around her and say to my mum
'why?'

I cant explain it son you see
The teachers here are great
No time to chat this morning, we'll end up being
late

And when mum starts to think what she really
wants to say
Is thanks to everyone who has gone out of their
way
The names are truly endless, but you know just
who you are
You're that very special person who shines out
like a star

The care at this school is second to none
The end of one chapter for my eldest son
The start of a new one at UCS
Am I crying, You bet I am, Yes

I

Daddy

I am a BROWN, your buster, and you Daddy are
my hero

Life is hard, love is dark but I remember all our
days

Swimming races, and the summer rays
You taught me love, to give and be kind

I know you loved me and I thank you for all
For what you taught me, I stand here tall

I am a woman, I am sad and strong
Daddy I still play our favourite song
Save all your kisses for me, The Brother Hood
of Man
I sing it in the car and as often as I can.

The Song Thief

Moo went the cow as he chewed on some hay
Oink went the pig as he went on his way
The dog went woof
And the bird looked at you
The Song Thief
Cockle Doodle Doo

The Sheep went Baa
The Duck went quack
The Horse went neigh

With his Nose in the sac
The cat went miaow
The chicks went cluck
The piglets drank
suck suck suck

So song thief
come look around
see the animals
hear their sound

Pigs in the sty
go grunt grunt grunt
chicks search for food
hunt hunt hunt

Sheep go Baa
Cats go Miaow
under the tree is the black and white cow
SO song thief come look around
See the animals
Hear their sounds

The Boy

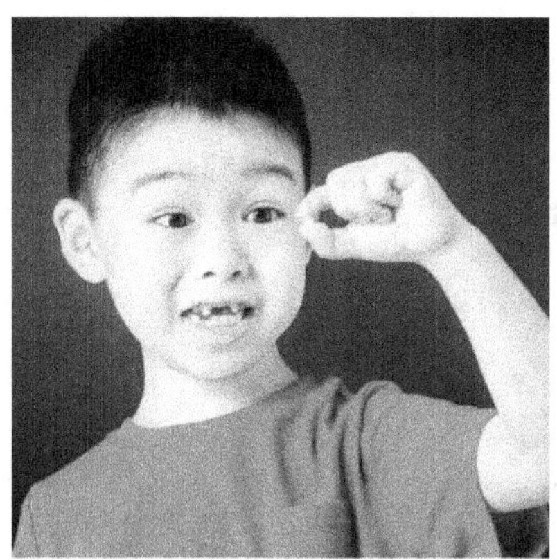

"My tooth is so wobbly
Why won't it budge
It didn't even fall out
When I ate my brother's fudge

I'm only six but I can't wait
I'll have to do it quick
It has to happen here and now
Or I will be quite sick."

My Mum keeps asking " what's the rush?
It's just a little tooth."

But I've been waiting patiently,
That really is the truth.

Nighttime comes and I count to three . . .
My fingers do the rest
Wibble, wobble, wibble.
I really try my best

The boy shouts "OUCH, I won't give up
I'll give a little tug"
Wibble,wobble,wibble
"I'm feeling rather smug"

"Hooray, Hooray I did it
The tooth now in my hand.
Time to meet Tallulah
Down in fairyland."

The Fairy Party

There on the star is Tallulah
So gracious as she waits
By her side Pixie sees
Fairy china plates

Libby Lilly squeals
She wakes the others too
But Ruby Rose still can't move
There's nothing she can do

Dawn begins the fairies stretch
They see the morning light
This tooth now in Tallulah's hand
Is a magic type of white

" I'm sorry I'm sorry"
 I truly am indeed
Ruby Rose was crying
She was desperate to be freed

Tallulah held her wand
She blinked her crystal eyes
Ruby Rose please promise now ..
There must be no more lies

I promise Queen Tallulah
I've learnt a lot tonight
No one likes a fairy
That always wants to fight....

The fairy pink ice cream
Was eaten with delight
The man in the moon winked again
For morning was his night....

Twenty Four

Looking back I see the pool
Turquoise water, oh so cool,
Our garden was amazing
My mother did her best
Making sure our flowers bloomed
Incase we had a guest

The lawn was neatly mowed
The tortoise loved it so
He was rather speedy
And often on the go

Summer times at 24
A child's dream come true
Table tennis, swimming, and always lots to do

They are the memories
I hold close to my heart
And as life unravelled
Our family fell apart

Those happy days dissolved
A memory they became
Life as I knew it was never the same

So treasure your days the good and the bad
Knowing life is a mix of happy and sad

Broken

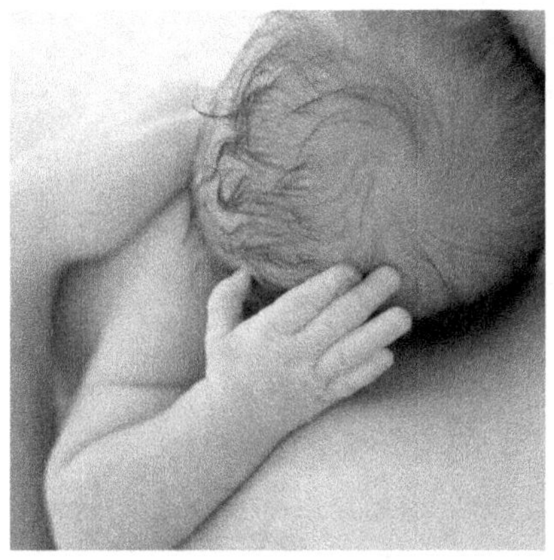

As my heart beat kept you alive
For 40 weeks we were one
You and me together
Me as your mother
You as my son

My beautiful stomach stretched out wide
So proud of the miracle
That I had inside
My strong spine held you
And I cherished each moment
Waiting for the day we were to meet

The day arrived, I was full of joy
Me your mother with my little boy
That moment I held you
I was never prepared
For the most incredible
Love affair of my life

You were the greatest gift
And I held you tight next to my chest
Skin to skin, I watched you rest
I gave you life, you gave me life

My heart then was whole, you were my door
To life, a life I dreamt of and now so long ago
that was
What happened to turn my life into such deep
sadness
Where did you go, I am looking for you,
I cannot see you anywhere , I'm filled with
panic

You have just gone and just like that
Like fairy dust, you were taken and now I know
You were never really mine

Who Am I

I am a woman who believes in LIFE
I am a woman who loves so deeply its painful
I am a woman who wanted to live life as ME

Why bring me here to change me
You are ashamed of the me that I am
But maybe what you see in me
Lacks in you

This I imagine makes you feel naked
Void of light
I cannot help you, I won't be your pain
This is my life not yours

You hurt me and I have allowed you to
Fire bullets into my throat
Finally, the last shot penetrated my heart
I fell down and died

It was over, you finally won
Your wish to lose me finally begun

But now I can see I am dead
There is a beam of light above my head

I can breathe without air
What has happened, I'm dead
I am reincarnating

You saved me with your bullet
I no longer feel your pain
I am starting my life
I survived and I am rising
Like the phonenix

Up I get, I stand now flooded in a new life
You did it, again you gave me life with your lies
I start again, for you I have no tears

Don't talk about me like I'm dead
I'm still me, but now you won't know this me
Just the angels see
It wasn't my time, I have more work to complete

I take my hand, hold me tight
I will lead you home and together
you will know, I am here for you,
Rise up with me, I'm with you

I was born to be free
Thank you for the lesson
It's time to be me

Mina

I will always be grateful
You were my heart
Not my blood
But that of another

You were my hero,
The survivor of atrocity
You held no hatred
Just pure love

Mina Minceberg you showed me the way
You gave me light and lit up my world

You were my second mother
Please keep me safe til we unite on the other
side of this life

Til we meet once more,
Wait for me, when I come, open that door and
Shower me with your warmth and love
I know you're helping from up above

I see you in my dreams and for that I am happy
My love to you stretches to wherever you are
A woman of worth, too good for earth

Until then...

Your sweetheart

When You Get A Thought Inside Your Head

And realise its a sign

That thought that sat patiently
For you to say… your mine

Searching for that extra piece,
The one that makes you whole
Can't be found in someone else
Only you can fill that role

So waking up at 4am, before the morning sun
That thought just tapped me gently

It's time that you begun

And gosh I know how true that is,
That thought just wants to stay
Till I have learned the lesson…
And I think that it's today

My body needs love and a well earned break
Time to relax and sit by a lake
My body is tired and I know I'm the one
The one responsible, so sit, don't run

Why do you run I ask my head
And I know the reason why

Hard to change my ways
So I sit, think and gaze
I take a deep breath.. exhale a slow long sigh
The thought in my head just asks me why

Why do you not care about me
I am you, can't you see

You need me, this body, to keep you alive
To keep you healthy so you can thrive

Life is so short, you say this to all
So now in your court I place the ball

The thought still here, it won't go now
My life will be, what I allow

For I am the boss, I make my rule
If I want to grow I am the fuel

So that thought, I must honestly say
Thank you for coming , you don't need to stay

I've now got the message, It's all down to me
My life in my hands… and I want to be free

It's time to unwrap the weight of the past
Why oh why did I put myself last

Because it's easier to help all of you
Stops me thinking of what I must do

If you ever think I have it down to a T
I haven't, I'm just like you, this person you see

And of course I'm brave and I'm strong
But it's taken years of practise, the road has been
long

It's worth it though, when you turn up for you
ONLY you can help you, harsh but true

Take the help, turn pain into hope
Turn wounds into wisdom, you will thrive, you
will cope

My journeys been exceptionally tough
Learn from my wins, take the smooth with the
rough

Keep showing up, make small steps each day
That's the answer to live life your way

You are unique, a gift to mankind
Honour yourself, take care of your mind

Your mind is your home, so treat it with care
Find your own tribe, let the rest stare

Be YOU every day, make You number one
Wake up with the bright morning sun

So back to my thought , I knew what you'd say
And yes, you are right, today is the day

www.ingramcontent.com/pod-product-compliance
Lightning Source LLC
Chambersburg PA
CBHW052337150726

47998CB00018B/2383